P9-DIE-712

BE LOVED

EMMA MAE JENKINS

New Growth Press, Greensboro, NC 27404
www.newgrowthpress.com
Copyright © 2019 by Emma Mae Jenkins

Unless otherwise indicated, Scripture quotations are taken from THE HOLY BIBLE, NEW INTERNATIONAL VERSION®, NIV® Copyright © 1973, 1978, 1984, 2011 by Biblica, Inc.® Used by permission. All rights reserved worldwide.

Scripture quotations marked AMP are taken from the Amplified Bible, Copyright © 2015 by The Lockman Foundation, La Habra, CA 90631. All rights reserved. For Permission To Quote information visit http://www.lockman.org/

Scripture quotations marked ESV are taken from The Holy Bible, English Standard Version.® Copyright © 2000; 2001 by Crossway Bibles, a division of Good News Publishers. Used by permission. All rights reserved.

Scripture quotations marked NLT are taken from Holy Bible, New Living Translation, copyright © 1996, 2004, 2015 by Tyndale House Foundation. Used by permission of Tyndale House Publishers, Inc., Carol Stream, Illinois 60188. All rights reserved.

Cover Design: Trish Mahoney, themahoney.com
Interior Design and Typesetting: Tom Temple, tandemcreative.net
Interior Photography: Delyn Stirewalt (page 19), Melissa Wise (page 110), all other photos by Mallory Zynda, malloryjophoto.com

ISBN: 978-1-948130-92-9

Library of Congress Cataloging-in-Publication Data

Names: Jenkins, Emma Mae, 1999- author.
Title: Be loved / Emma Mae Jenkins.
Description: Greensboro : New Growth Press, 2019. | Audience: Ages 11-16 |
  Description: Greensboro : New Growth Press, 2019. | Audience: Ages 11-16 |
  Audience: Grades 7-9 | Summary: "Emma Mae Jenkins, a young writer, has
  inspired many with the freedom she has to be herself-a dearly loved
  child of God. In her first book, Be Loved, she invites readers to join
  her on a journey of life-changing faith and the freedom that comes from
  knowing the love of God. She chronicles her own high school journey
  through starting a new school, navigating the typical pressures of
  school work and sports, going to prom, and even homecoming. Emma Mae
  faced each new challenge with the confidence that God was with her and
  was going to make her uniquely useful in the place he had prepared for
  her. For Emma Mae, it all starts with her relationship with Jesus.
  Because she knows she is loved by him, she is free to be herself and to
  live out her faith no matter what the cost. As a young, passionate, and
  intimate lover of Jesus, Emma Mae's love for her Savior overflows
  unashamedly into her unconditional, fierce love for people. Readers will
  experience the chain-breaking liberty of knowing the Lord's presence and
  the freedom to be unique. This full-color, hardback book includes
  pictures from Emma Mae's life, along with key Bible verses that God used
  to strengthen and guide her through the ups and downs of her high school
  years. Readers will learn to face the challenges of their student years
  with faith, courage, hope, and lifegiving love for others"-- Provided by
  publisher.
Identifiers: LCCN 2019026081 | ISBN 9781948130929 (hardcover)
Subjects: LCSH: Christian teenagers--Religious life--Juvenile literature. |
  Preteens--Religious life--Juvenile literature. | God
  (Christianity)--Love--Juvenile literature. | Grace (Theology)--Juvenile
  literature.
Classification: LCC BV4531.3 .J46 2019 | DDC 248.8/3--dc23
LC record available at https://lccn.loc.gov/2019026081

Printed in Malaysia   26 25 24 23 22 21 20 19   1 2 3 4 5

CONTENTS

FOREWORD >>>

Emma Jenkins is a walking ray of sunshine whose light radiates the love of Jesus everywhere she goes. It doesn't matter if Emma is speaking in front of thousands of people, posting on social media, or with you one on one, her joy and genuine, positive spirit remain the same. She is no different than any other ordinary young adult, except she has decided to find herself fully in Christ alone, and that is what makes her the extraordinary young woman that she is.

One of my favorite things about Emma is her love for the Word of God. On my very first Live Original tour, Emma taught me the armor of God. She walked me through it, acting it out as she put on each piece of armor.

Many people want to know Scripture and be able to recite it so effortlessly, as Emma does, and as her friend, I can tell you the reason she is able to do that is because she has truly immersed herself in the Word; even her bedroom is covered in Scripture. By reading this book, your desire to learn Scripture will deepen, and you will fall in love with the Word of God.

Emma shares powerful verses that speak truth over some of our most commonly believed lies. The illustrations in the book and her sweet spirit make it a fun read, but it's so much more than just a fun read. Emma addresses, head-on, some of the toughest and most relatable challenges teenagers face on a daily basis. She invites you in with her transparency and vulnerability as she shares her own stories and leads you to discover your own truth and identity in Jesus. Like Emma, I am passionate about young people becoming confident in their own original identity for which God has created for them. It's so easy for us to go through identity crises during our middle school, high school, and college years. It's especially an issue now with social media, bullying, and the world telling you that you should be everything opposite of who God created you to be. As hard as it can be, I hope by picking up this book, you already know you are not alone. You have two sisters in Emma and me, walking right there with you.

I believe if you take hold of the advice Emma gives in this book, let the scriptures she provides take root in your heart, and pray alongside her the prayers she walks you through, you will be led straight to finding your identity in Christ.

You will become confident in the person you were created to be, because you will have fallen in love with the creator himself.

I truly believe role models can be younger than you, and I am proud to say Emma is one of my role models. She has inspired my love for God's word and prayer, which are two of the most powerful things you can have in life. I know Emma's heart would be to sit down with every single one of you and have a cup of tea. Since she may not be able to do that, I know she has put every ounce of truth and wisdom into a book that is wrapped in love and filled with joy, just for you!

Sadie Robertson

For it is by grace you have been saved, through faith—and this is not from yourselves, it is the gift of God—not by works, so that no one can boast. Ephesians 2:8-9

CHAPTER ONE

BE LOVED.
Be Free.

I grew up in a home that loved the Lord, and I don't remember a time when I didn't believe in and love Jesus.

VERY EARLY ON I DELIGHTED IN HIM AND WAS OVERCOME BY HIS INEXPRESSIBLE AND GLORIOUS JOY. AS A FAMILY WE WENT TO CHURCH EVERY SUNDAY, AND I WAS VERY INVOLVED WITH MY YOUTH GROUP.

I LOVED PEOPLE, AND I LOVED LIFE.

BUT EVEN THOUGH I KNEW **GOD LOVED ME,**

SOMEHOW I STILL THOUGHT I HAD TO EARN HIS LOVE EVERY DAY.

HOW I VIEWED MYSELF IS AN IMPORTANT PART OF THIS STORY.

I tried to be gracious and kind and loving toward everyone I met, but I wasn't gracious or kind or loving toward myself.

You see,
I had set the
standard of
perfection upon
myself. **Let's**
pause
here.

No one else set that standard
on me. I chose to believe I had to be perfect to earn love.
I was afraid of messing up, and I worried that I wasn't
good enough. If I messed up, would my
reputation be ruined? What
would God think of me?

I didn't want to admit to myself that I was afraid, but I was.
I was afraid that my best efforts would not be enough to
please my friends, my parents, and maybe especially God.

In trying to be perfect, I set a standard for myself
I couldn't meet. I was constantly burdened by my
feeling that I could never be enough or do enough.

One night I felt so overwhelmed by trying to be perfect and to please everyone that I laid down on my bed and cried. Anxious thoughts held me captive. I knew that I should listen to God's words instead of my own thoughts, but I just didn't know how to do that. My dad found me in my room, lying on my bed and crying in exhaustion. I was worn out and afraid to be myself—even to the point of not wanting to move because it would be an imperfect movement. Fear paralyzed me. I felt completely drained. My dad asked me what was wrong, and I shared with him how burdened I was. He pointed to the Bible on my bookshelf and gently asked me when I last spent time with Jesus in his word. I wanted to answer him honestly, so I sat in silence trying to think. But I couldn't remember. I mean, I loved Jesus and we went to church every Sunday, but I could not recall the last time I went to a quiet place to be alone with God and his word.

DRAINED worn
OVERWHELMED listen
nxious
EXHAUSTION captiv

My dad went on to tell me that when Jesus returns again, I will not be standing there in the presence of Jesus on judgment day with my dad, holding his hand. It will be just Jesus and me, and my faith can't be my dad's faith. Jesus will either tell me,

Well done

GOOD AND FAITHFUL SERVANT

MATTHEW 25:23

or DEPART *from me*

FOR I NEVER KNEW YOU.

MATTHEW 7:21-23

Then my dad reminded me that I didn't have to do everything perfectly or check off a specific number of boxes or make a certain number of people happy for Jesus to welcome me. Jesus simply says he will only tell us to depart from him if he never knew us.

Overwhelmed by the power of this truth, I was in awe. Jesus wants to know me! Jesus wants me to know him! He is jealous for us to not just know of him, but to genuinely know him. And to enter into this relationship, we are not required to be enough. Jesus was enough when we, in our sin, could not be. I can try to be good and do the right thing all of my days and still not be good enough to enter into a relationship with God on my own meril. All of the sudden, I got it! It's okay that I'm not enough. Jesus is enough for me.

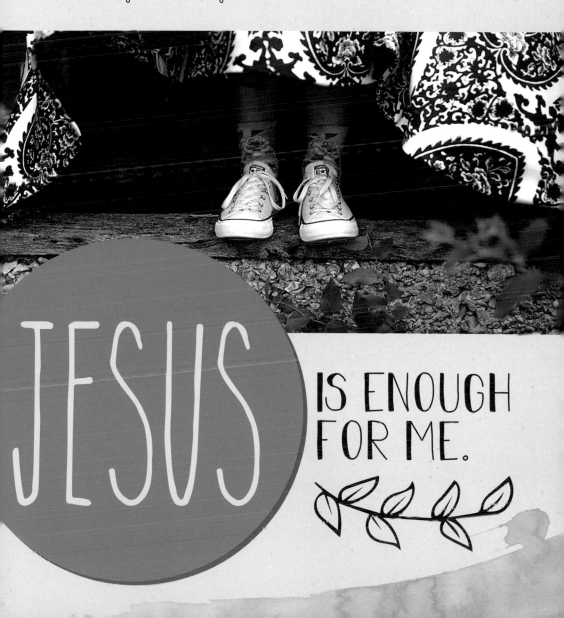

JESUS IS ENOUGH FOR ME.

EPHESIANS 2:8

tells us that by grace we have been saved, through faith, and this is not by works so no one can boast. God so loved me and you that he sent Jesus, his one and only Son, to come and die for us so if we believe in him, we shall not perish, but have eternal life (John 3:16). "God demonstrates his own love for us in this: While we were still sinners, Christ died for us" (Romans 5:8).

We put our hope in so many different things to try and earn the love each of us desperately craves. This comes in many different forms, but the root of our striving is that we all desire to be loved, and this desire was knitted fearfully and wonderfully in the depths of our hearts by Love himself. Only he can be the one to fill it. To be in relationship with Jesus is to be saved from our sins that lead to death, to have hope that can't be stolen, and to walk in the full confidence that nothing in all of creation can separate us from his love (Romans 8:39). It's so beautifully simple. He just wants our hearts. He wants us to put all our trust in him.

To be fully his is to be fully free to discover the beautiful you he so delightfully made you to be—not to look like the world, but like him instead. Being different isn't easy, but it's worth it. I've learned I would much rather be free in his love than be trapped in the exhausting cycle of seeking the approval of others.

"God demonstrates His perfect love for us in that while we were still sinners, Christ died for us." Romans 5:8

PRAY

When I try to earn your love—the gift of your love—remind my heart that I can't and I don't have to. Help me to live in the freedom of Christ's love for me so that out of that love, I can be gracious and kind toward everyone, including myself.

When I am paralyzed by the fear of messing up and feel like I have to be perfect, turn my eyes to Jesus, who met that standard of perfection on the cross so I don't have to.

When I am burdened by feeling I could never be enough or do enough, show me Jesus, who is sufficient of all things (2 Corinthians 9:8).

When I do fail or when I'm discouraged, put your Word on my lips to encourage me. Surround me with friends and family who point to Jesus over and over again.

When I want to go my own way and hide from you, draw me closer to yourself. Help me to run to you with my concerns, failures, and fears.

When I'm afraid to approach you with my failures, help me to remember you demonstrate your perfect love for me in that while I was still a sinner, you died for me (Romans 5:8). Nothing can separate me from your love (Romans 8:38-39).

SCRIPTURE TO REMEMBER

"Humble yourselves, therefore, under God's mighty hand, that he may lift you up in due time. Cast all your anxiety on him because he cares for you" (1 Peter 5:6-7).

"For if, while we were God's enemies, we were reconciled to him through the death of his Son, how much more, having been reconciled, shall we be saved through his life!" (Romans 5:10).

"There is no fear in love. But perfect love drives out fear, because fear has to do with punishment. The one who fears is not made perfect in love" (1 John 4:18).

"But because of his great love for us, God, who is rich in mercy, made us alive with Christ even when we were dead in transgressions—it is by grace you have been saved" (Ephesians 2:4-5).

" In all these things we are more than conquerors through him who loved us. For I am convinced that neither death nor life, neither angels nor demons, neither the present nor the future, nor any powers, neither height nor depth, nor anything else in all creation, will be able to separate us from the love of God that is in Christ Jesus our Lord" (Romans 8:37-39).

"THEREFORE, THERE IS NOW NO CONDEMNATION FOR THOSE WHO ARE IN CHRIST JESUS, BECAUSE THROUGH CHRIST JESUS THE LAW OF THE SPIRIT WHO GIVES LIFE HAS SET YOU FREE FROM THE LAW OF SIN AND DEATH" (ROMANS 8:1-2).

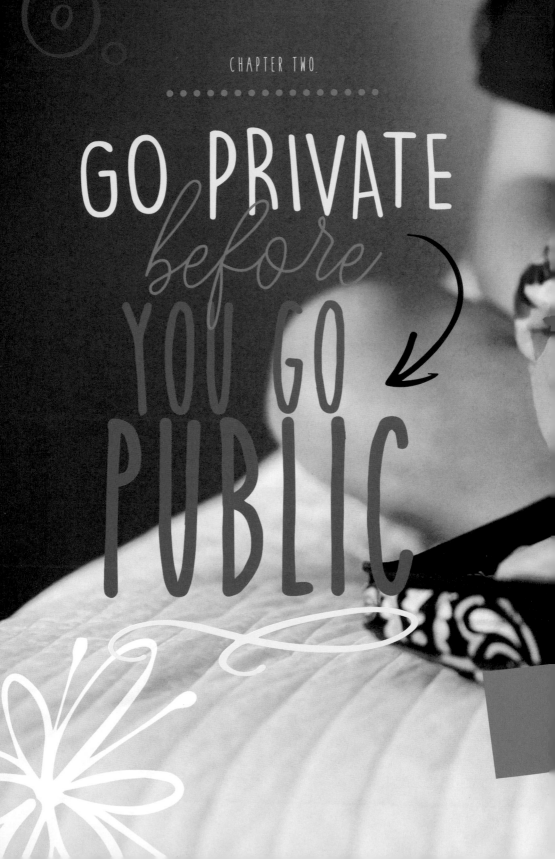

CHAPTER TWO

GO PRIVATE *before* YOU GO PUBLIC

Let the morning bring me word of Your unfailing love, for I put my trust in You. Show me the way I should go, for to You I entrust my life; rescue me from my enemies, for I hide myself in You. Teach me to do Your will, for You are my God, may Your good Spirit lead me on level ground. Psalm 143:8-10

GROWING UP, I MOVED MANY TIMES,

so I had to change schools often, which meant meeting new people and making new friends. Making friends usually means stepping outside of our comfort zones to get to know and be known by others. Sometimes that means being a little bit uncomfortable.

I will never forget the time I moved from Florida to Alabama. I went to a big youth event one Wednesday night at the church our family ended up joining. I walked into the auditorium with my mom and brother and saw at least a thousand students. With my big, bright, and very blue bow high up in my ponytail, I bravely told my mom I was going to go and find a friend. I left the comfort of my mom's side and set out into the crowd to see where God wanted me to sit.

I walked down the aisle and scanned the rows one by one. Eventually, I came across a row with two lovely girls. I asked if I could have the honor of sitting with them. They had the sweetest smiles and gladly welcomed me to sit next to them. I found out that they were sisters. The older sister, Amanda, was in high school, and the younger sister, Caroline, was my age and was also about to enter the eighth grade! I love the small, but wonderful ways God orchestrates everything. He is so fun and kind, and he delights in the details. He will never lead us to a place where he is absent. God has already made a way.

We worshipped together and listened to God's Word, and then we exchanged phone numbers so we could stay in touch. The first day of school rolled around, and I woke up that morning to a text message from Caroline. She had sent me a devotional to encourage me! All through that year, then through high school, and now even in college, our friendship has deepened and blossomed. Even when I moved eight hours away from her, we continued to stay in touch. She is still one of my best friends.

HE WILL NEVER LEAD US TO A PLACE WHERE HE IS ABSENT

Why am I telling you this story? Because we all know many people, but to truly know someone takes investment. If I want to grow closer to someone, I must spend time with that person. To build and cultivate a relationship, we have to be intentional. My friendship with Caroline would not have grown and deepened if we had we not continued to talk with each other and spend time together and make our friendship a priority.

THE SAME IS TRUE OF OUR RELATIONSHIP WITH JESUS.

A relationship with Jesus always brings us out of our comfort zone. We can't really get to know Jesus unless we are willing to leave where we are and follow him. As we follow him, we can taste and see his love and freedom in ways we never could have imagined. A relationship with him is not of this world, so it's not going to fit the mold of what culture says is normal.

Just as I walked down the aisle with my bright and quite large blue bow with excitement and uncertainty, walking with Jesus is going to feel odd and uncertain sometimes — but because you are walking with him, you will have a confidence that cannot be stolen. This means our comfort zone has to be set aside. To step out of our comfort zone toward Jesus is to step into peace that surpasses all understanding. Just as my relationship with Caroline took time to grow, our relationship with Jesus is not fully built on one experience; it takes spending time together daily. It's a daily walk, hand in hand with him.

What does that look like for me? My time with God affects how I spend my time in every other moment of the day. In Matthew 6:33, Jesus said to seek him and his kingdom first, so I choose to daily give the first of my day to him. He is worthy of my first. Jesus also did this with the Father.

VERY EARLY IN THE MORNING, WHILE IT WAS STILL DARK, JESUS GOT UP, LEFT THE HOUSE AND WENT OFF TO A SOLITARY PLACE, WHERE HE PRAYED.

MARK 1:35

Jesus wants us to imitate him in how we live (1 John 2:6). So I wake up early in the morning, before school, and go to a quiet place to be with him before I'm with anyone else. This is not always comfortable, but it's worth it. As Pastor Chris Hodges says, „Before I check my social media, I am looking to God's media." It is essential.

TO STEP OUT OF OUR COMFORT ZONE TOWARD JESUS IS TO STEP INTO PEACE THAT SURPASSES ALL UNDERSTANDING.

As my eyes open, I am so thankful I get to belong to God! "From the rising of the sun to its setting, the name of the LORD is to be praised" (Psalm 113:3). I wake up in awe that I can praise him, so I start singing

as I dangle my feet off my bed.

From my head to my toes, I give him my thoughts and everywhere my feet will go. The song of my heart before I set my feet on the ground is captured in Psalm 143:8-10:

LET THE MORNING BRING ME WORD OF YOUR UNFAILING LOVE, FOR I PUT MY TRUST IN YOU. SHOW ME THE WAY I SHOULD GO, FOR TO YOU I ENTRUST MY LIFE. RESCUE ME FROM MY ENEMIES, LORD, FOR I HIDE MYSELF IN YOU. TEACH ME TO DO YOUR WILL, FOR YOU ARE MY GOD. MAY YOUR GOOD SPIRIT LEAD ME ON LEVEL GROUND.

I turn my lamp on to remind me of his Word, which is a lamp to my feet and a light to my path (Psalm 119:105).

Then, I go to the foot of my bed, which is my prayer place. This is not the only place I pray-prayer is unceasing!-but this is a designated spot I go to be with God.

"Because he bends down to listen, I will pray as long as I have breath!" (Psalm 116:2 NLT). Being watchful and thankful (Colossians 4:2), I spend this time talking to God and listening to him. He is my best friend and Lord, so to be with him is to be in reverent awe and joyful comfort all at once.

After a time of prayer,
I open up his Word.

The Bible is truth, and it's so important to know who he is and who he says I am, because I know the moment I walk out of my door to enter the day, I will be told many lies about who he is and who I am. His Word is where my identity is found and rooted, and the more I spend time with him in his Word, the more I become familiar with the sound of his voice. In John 10, we are told that Jesus is the Good Shepherd who calls his sheep by name, and his sheep follow him because they know the sound of his voice. But the sheep will never follow a stranger; in fact, they will run away because they do not recognize a stranger's voice.

HIS WORD IS WHERE MY IDENTITY IS FOUND AND ROOTED, AND THE MORE I SPEND TIME WITH HIM IN HIS WORD, THE MORE I BECOME FAMILIAR WITH THE SOUND OF HIS VOICE.

I must go private with the Good Shepherd, so I can follow his voice of truth and recognize the voice of deceit when in public. Sometimes my time in his Word looks like meditating on one verse, while other mornings it looks like reading a whole chapter. Both types of mornings are just as powerful because they are with him. When I have spent time with him in the Bible, I turn on my "Jesus Jams" playlist and sing and dance and praise him. In secret, we have a praise party, and what is done privately overflows publicly.

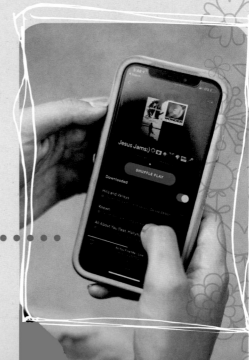

Relationships are unique.

Meeting many different people as I grew up moving from place to place meant my friendships were special each in their own way. Each precious soul I got to know was original, and our time together didn't look like my time with someone else. In a similar way, my relationship with Jesus is not going to look like a spitting image of your relationship with him, and that is awesome! As you read about my private time with the Lord, know that it's unique to my personal relationship with him. Your private time with him does not have to look exactly like mine, it simply must consist of prayer, his Word, and worship, and how you dance through that with him is unique. Enjoy this vital time with him and how it deepens your intimate relationship and deep love for him.

Right now, wherever you are, is the perfect place to begin stepping out of your comfort zone toward a deeper intimacy with Jesus. "Do not despise these small beginnings, for the LORD rejoices to see the work begin" (Zechariah 4:10 NLT). Sometimes we believe the enemy's lie that because we haven't been spending time with God and seeking him first, there's no way we can measure up. But that is a lie. Jesus is calling you by name and he loves you. Or perhaps you are hearing the lie that God does not want you to be with him because you have been ignoring him. But this is not the heart of your heavenly Father. He is jealous for you and desires to be sought by you and never will he leave you or forsake you (Exodus 20:5; Deuteronomy 31:6).

I long to be with him and crave time with him—not because it will give me more brownie points with Jesus—but simply because I want to grow closer to him. When you walk daily with him, hand in hand, you will begin to publicly make known your love for Jesus to others who are observing your life. Others will notice that your walk looks different because of who you are walking with.

DO NOT DESPISE
THESE SMALL BEGINNINGS
FOR THE LORD REJOICES TO SEE
THE WORK BEGIN

Zechariah 4:10

✤✤PRAY✤✤

When I am nervous or anxious to meet new people or be intentional in my relationships, help me to step outside of my comfort zone to get to know and be known by others so I can see and taste your love and freedom.

When I am afraid to approach others, help me to know you are guiding me and you are with me. Help me to stand in the confidence I have in you and your peace that surpasses all understanding.

When I doubt that you are with me, help me to remember you delight in the details, and you love the slow process of change. Help me to trust that you orchestrate everything, and that you never leave me or forsake me.

When I strive to be intentional to build and cultivate my relationship with you and others, help me to show up consistently, trusting that you do the work. Remind me of your relentless love and pursuit of the ones you love, that I might model that love in my relationship with others.

When I am discouraged about spending time with you, remind me that I don't have to "clean myself up" before I come to you. Help me to know you meet me where I am, and I can grow in my relationship with you regardless of my struggles and shortcomings. Protect me from the lie that you don't want to spend time with me because of _____.

When I seek you, help me to creatively and wisely carve out intentional time to praise you in the way you created me to praise you: by meditating on your Word, worshiping you, and praying to you. Just as Jesus sought the Father and his kingdom first, I can choose to daily give the first of my day to you.

When I am told lies about who you are and who I am, fill my mind and heart with your Word, which is truth. Help me to soak in your Bible, where my identity is found. Thank you for being the Good Shepherd. Help me to follow your voice of truth and recognize the voice of deceit.

When I walk daily with God and spend time with him privately, help me to be an outward display of your love for all people. Thank you that you promise to go before me.

✦✦✦

SCRIPTURE TO REMEMBER

"Do not fear, for I am with you; do not be dismayed, for I am your God. I will strengthen you and help you; I will uphold you with my righteous hand" (Isaiah 41:10).

"He is before all things, and in him all things hold together" (Colossians 1:17).

"Then Jesus came to them and said, 'All authority in heaven and on earth has been given to me. Therefore go and make disciples of all nations, baptizing them in the name of the Father and of the Son and of the Holy Spirit, and teaching them to obey everything I have commanded you. And surely I am with you always, to the very end of the age.'" (Matthew 28:18-20).

"Very early in the morning, while it was still dark, Jesus got up, left the house and went off to a solitary place, where he prayed" (Mark 1:35).

"Do not despise these small beginnings, for the LORD rejoices to see the work begin" (Zechariah 4:10 NLT).

"FROM THE RISING OF THE SUN TO THE PLACE WHERE IT SETS, THE NAME OF THE LORD IS TO BE PRAISED" (PSALM 113:3).

There is no fear in love. But perfect love drives out fear, because fear has to do with punishment. The one who fears is not made perfect in love. 1 John 4:18

CHAPTER THREE

WALKING *the* HALLS

A s we unpacked the moving boxes one more time, I sat down for a moment in our new home and realized that I was so scared. The new school year was quickly approaching. The summer before my tenth-grade year, our family moved from Alabama to Arkansas, and this would be my fifth time to be the "new girl." Fear was heavy, loneliness pressed down on my heart as tears filled my eyes and I cried out to God. Simply crying out to him with complete honesty brought me comfort. I knew my heavenly Father was there. I could not say that I was excited about moving again, but I can tell you with complete certainty that I was expectant of the beauty God had in store for me—which would blow me away because that is who God is.

fear WAS HEAVY *loneliness* PRESSED DOWN ON MY HEART

Whenever I have moved to a new place, it always takes a while for people to grasp that I am being genuine. Initially, a lot of people are confused and don't know how to respond to me. They think my joy and kindness is fake, and I knew this rocky start was waiting for me at a new school. I was afraid I was not going to make any friends. I called my Momma to come upstairs, and I shared with her what was going on in my heart and talked it through with her. She reminded me that God would never call us to a place he hasn't gone before us, and he had prepared the way for us.

GOD SINGS TO OUR HEARTS THE TRUTH OF HEBREWS 13:5, NEVER WILL I LEAVE YOU; NEVER WILL I FORSAKE YOU.

This wisdom that flowed from her heart was so encouraging, and I began to rest in it.

The first day of school was nearing, and the Holy Spirit transitioned my focus from fear to love. I realized I was full of fear because I was focused on myself. Love is not self-seeking, and because I was focusing on Emma and whether or not I was going to make friends and what others were going to think of me, I was not able to operate out of love. His perfect love casts out all fear. So instead of fixing my gaze on myself, I looked to Jesus and found myself giddy about the opportunity to love his people at my new high school of forty-five hundred students.

PERFECT LOVE
-CASTS OUT-
ALL FEAR

LOVE

THE NIGHT BEFORE SCHOOL STARTED I COULDN'T SLEEP BECAUSE I WAS SO EXCITED ABOUT WHAT GOD HAD IN STORE FOR THIS NEW SEASON OF LIFE. I BEGAN TO PRAY OVER ALL OF THE STUDENTS I HAD NOT YET MET, THE STUDENTS AT THE SCHOOLS I HAD BEEN TO IN THE PAST, MY FAMILY, AND EVEN MY FUTURE HUSBAND. I SENT OUT OVER ONE HUNDRED TEXT MESSAGES TO ALMOST EVERYONE I KNEW, ENCOURAGING THEM IN TRUTH AS THEY WERE ABOUT TO ENTER INTO THEIR NEW SCHOOL YEAR TOO. IT WAS ALMOST AS IF CHRISTMAS WAS THE NEXT MORNING. TO LIVE IN THE LOVE OF JESUS IS TO BE FREE FROM FEAR. BECAUSE I KNEW GOD WAS EXCITED ABOUT TOMORROW, I HAD EVERY REASON TO BE EXCITED TOO.

As the sun came up, God's peace that surpasses all understanding surrounded me like a shield and filled every part of me (Philippians 4:7). I curled my hair and was so ready because I knew God had exceedingly and abundantly greater things in store than what I could ever ask or imagine (Ephesians 3:20).

WHILE WALKING THROUGH THE UNFAMILIAR HALLWAYS, I WAS AMAZED.

When you begin to see yourself the way God sees you, you can't help but begin to see others the way God sees them. Every person I saw excited me because they were each uniquely beautiful. Because our mouths speak from that which fills our hearts, I couldn't help but declare out loud this truth to each person. It's very important to not let our actions be determined by how we think other people will react. If I would have stopped to think about people's reactions, I wouldn't have the confidence to tell people how beautiful they were. But perfect love truly does cast out all fear (1 John 4:18). Because I was operating out of God's love, I was able to freely love people regardless of how they responded. Some reacted with joy and graciousness while others were skeptical and hesitant.

Going through the process of moving, STARTING A NEW SCHOOL, and making new friends required immense patience. It takes time for people to get to know one another, and I enjoyed getting to know the people at my new school and allowing them to get to know me. CULTIVATING RELATIONSHIPS with people is not easy, but it's WORTH IT and opens doors to share HOPE.

TO LIVE IN THE LOVE OF JESUS IS TO BE FREE FROM FEAR.

After attending this new school for about a year and a half, God reminded my heart while on Thanksgiving break,

Treat others the way you would want to be treated (Luke 6:31).

With joyful obedience, I dwelt in his word and began to think about how I would want to be treated. This simple thought came to my mind:

> It would be so wonderful to receive a Christmas card.

"All right, let's go get index cards at the store."

I welcomed this idea, and it began to grow. Why, exactly, would I love to receive a Christmas card? I knew it would be so sweet to receive one knowing someone was thinking about me and wanted me to know I was loved. This was how I wanted everyone at my school to feel! The Lord continued to paint his thoughts in my mind, and I had the idea of giving every student in my high school a Christmas card so they would each know they were thought of and loved. This was perfect! Possibly, this was the only Christmas card some of these students had ever received. Possibly, this would be the only time some of these students had ever heard the truth that they are loved.

Knowing this was from God's heart, I shared this idea with my mom. Immediately she said, "All right, let's go get index cards at the store." I love my mom. She was so willing to join me in this vision even though it was a ginormous task. She had confidence that because it was from God, he would help us do it. Once we had bought thousands of index cards, I reached out to all of the people God had blessed me to build relationships with. Isn't that funny? When I trusted God had me where he wanted me to be and I began to operate out of the freedom of his love, he used the exact thing I was once afraid of to propel the vision he had given me. I texted the girls on my soccer team, people in my youth group, and people in clubs I was involved in. We ended up having about forty people come over to our house to help make Christmas cards. It was so fun, and I was awestruck that God gave provision for his vision. People helped us, and we made cards leading up to the week before Christmas break. After making almost four thousand Christmas cards, a team of us distributed a card to each student in the high school. Some still have them to this day, while others threw them away as they walked out the door. But how sweet is it that the truth of God's love was shared with all of them? I love how God did not ask me to make Christmas cards as soon as I moved to Arkansas, but rather, he led me to patiently build relationships with people. God wants to free us in his love, so we can freely love others.

BECAUSE OF THE
unfailing love of God,

I was free to walk into the hallways
of a place I had never been to

meet and love people

I had never seen because I knew God had gone
ahead of me and prepared the way.

me & mom

PRAY

When fear is heavy and loneliness presses in around my heart, help me to cry out to you, God. Remind my heart that you are the God of comfort and peace, and you are always with me.

When I'm full of doubt, help me to rest in the truth that you will never leave me or forsake me. By your spirit, transition my focus from fear to love. Love is not self-seeking; show me how to walk in your perfect love, which casts out fear.

When I am trying to love others the way you love me, help me to fix my gaze on Jesus, not myself. Give me the compassion and mind of Christ to pursue others in freedom, not fear. Help me to see myself and others the way you see me and others.

When I am nervous how people might respond to me or my outward expression of faith, help me to operate out of God's love, not a fear of what others might think of me. Remind me of the confidence and indestructible hope I have in Jesus.

When I am ready to see change in my own life and relationships, grant me patience, and help me to lean on you. With joyful obedience, help me to remember cultivating relationships is not easy, but it opens doors to share hope.

When I am struggling with patience, help me to remember that you are leading me, and you have more in store for me than I could ever dare imagine or hope for.

>=·=<

SCRIPTURE TO REMEMBER

"Be completely humble and gentle; be patient, bearing with one another in love. Make every effort to keep the unity of the Spirit through the bond of peace" (Ephesians 4:2-3).

"Do not be anxious about anything, but in every situation, by prayer and petition, with thanksgiving, present your requests to God" (Philippians 4:6).

"Praise be to the God and Father of our Lord Jesus Christ, the Father of compassion and the God of all comfort, who comforts us in all our troubles, so that we can comfort those in any trouble with the comfort we ourselves receive from God" (2 Corinthians 1:3-4).

"There is no fear in love. But perfect love drives out fear" (1 John 4:18).

"'Never will I leave you; never will I forsake you'" (Hebrews 13:5).

"DO TO OTHERS AS YOU WOULD HAVE THEM DO TO YOU" (LUKE 6:31).

"Be joyful in hope, patient in affliction, faithful in prayer. Share with the Lord's people who are in need. Practice hospitality" (Romans 12:12-13).

"Peace I leave with you; my peace I give you. I do not give to you as the world gives. Do not let your hearts be troubled and do not be afraid" (John 14:27).

CHAPTER FOUR

LUNCH

Walking with purpose through the cafeteria one day, I approached a puddle of chocolate milk that was on the floor and, yes, I continued to walk with purpose straight into the puddle. I fell on my bumper in the cafeteria and began to laugh at myself.

But if anyone obeys his word, love for God is truly made complete in them. This is how we know we are in him: Whoever claims to live in him must live as Jesus did. I John 2:5-6

IT'S IMPORTANT
THAT WE ARE SERIOUS
ABOUT WHAT WE DO, BUT THAT
WE DO NOT TAKE OURSELVES TOO SERIOUSLY.

Getting right back up and walking right on, the Lord reminded me of the freedom he gives that enables us to keep on walking.

I am always hungry,

so during the school day, I would eat every hour. I brought my lunchbox with me to school and would eat one thing in each class. By the time lunch came, I had nothing left in my lunchbox. So, I would take "laps" through the cafeteria. Approaching each table, I met many original souls. Some were very talented in the athletic department, and others could play instruments like it was nobody's

business. Some of them were loud while others kept to themselves. My goodness, they were all so beautiful! During these laps, I would make my way to each table throughout the lunchroom and tell people how loved they are and ask them how they were doing. Some were thankful and engaged in a conversation with me, while others were caught off guard and hesitant, unsure why I was talking with them. With purpose, I got to keep walking from one table to the next to let people know that they were seen.

Some of my very favorite lunches were those when I saw people who did not have a lunch buddy, and I would have the honor of asking them if I could join them. Some told me they preferred to sit alone and others welcomed me to sit with them. One day in particular, I remember looking to see who the Lord wanted me to sit with, and I caught a glance from a beautiful girl sitting alone in the hallway eating by herself. I walked up to her and we began talking. I asked her if she wanted a lunch buddy, and she denied it by declaring no one ever wanted to sit beside her. Deeply burdened by the sense of rejection she seemed to dwell in, I got to explain to her how much I wanted to sit with her. She did let me join her, and we ate our yummy food together. To this day, she is a friend of mine. To be the hands and feet of Jesus, we have to deny ourselves, and he will use us to be vessels of his comfort to those who do not know him.

IN JOHN 4,

Jesus is traveling from Judea to Galilee, and we are told he "had to go through Samaria," but he did not have to go through Samaria to get to Galilee. The Jews despised the Samaritans and would walk around Samaria to get from Judea to Galilee simply so they could avoid encountering the Samaritans. But Jesus, the Jew, chose to go through the exact town his own people avoided because he knew a woman was there who had a hurting heart. He had to go through Samaria because he had to share hope with her. He went to the well to be with her and meet her where she was.

TO WALK IN THE FREEDOM OF CHRIST

is to walk in the direction that the rest of the crowd may not be walking in.

THE LUNCHROOM WAS MY SAMARIA.

Each table was my well, and because of what Jesus did, I went to the wells to meet people where they were.

·····························

In Acts 4, Peter and John were put in jail because they were proclaiming the good news of Jesus. The next day the rulers, elders, and teachers of the law brought Peter and John before them to question them saying, "By what power or what name did you do this?" (Acts 4:7). With boldness, Peter told them it was by the name of Jesus. "When they saw the courage of Peter and John and realized that they were unschooled, ordinary men, they were astonished, and they took note that these men had been with Jesus" (Acts 4:13).

"BUT IF ANYONE OBEYS HIS WORD, LOVE FOR GOD IS TRULY MADE COMPLETE IN THEM. THIS IS HOW WE KNOW THAT WE ARE IN HIM; WHOEVER CLAIMS TO LIVE IN HIM MUST LIVE AS JESUS DID."

1 JOHN 2:5-6

IN THE SAME WAY, WHEN WE WALK INTO THE LUNCHROOM AS A FORGIVEN AND FREE CHILD OF GOD,

people will see our courage and take note that we have been with Jesus. People will not take note that we have been with Jesus because of how much education we have or the amount of accomplishments we have—but simply by how we walk in love. They will see that we have the courage to love out of an overflow of how loved we are by him and how much we love him. After Jesus met with the woman at the well, she went into the town to tell the people about what Jesus just did in her life. Telling others what Jesus has done for us is as simple as walking into the lunchroom to share Jesus with the people we find there. People will take note that we have been with him. People will know we are his by our love (John 13:35).

Not every day is the same. Some days will look like falling in chocolate milk as we are walking with purpose in love, but because God is with us and he picks us up, we can keep walking, and he will use those moments to pick up other people too.

∾≋∞ PRAY ੦ৎৎ

When I walk with purpose, help me to not take myself too seriously but to delight in the freedom you give me to keep on walking.

When I approach others in the hallway, the cafeteria, or anywhere else, help me to be the hands and feet of Jesus and a vessel of your comfort to those who don't know him.

When I seek to live a life of faith, give me the confidence to boldly walk in the direction others aren't walking in, knowing you are with me.

When I am intentional about loving others, grant me the courage to love out of an overflow of your love for me. By your Spirit, help me to walk with purpose.

When I fall down or I fail others, remind my heart that you are my strength, and you will pick me up and others too. Help me to persevere in your calling for my life.

When I am concerned about what others think, keep my eyes on you, Jesus. Even when it's not the "popular" choice, help me to walk in the freedom of Christ, knowing you promise to meet me and go before me.

❧ SCRIPTURE TO REMEMBER ❧

"But if anyone obeys his word, love for God is truly made complete in them. This is how we know we are in him: Whoever claims to live in him must live as Jesus did" (1 John 2:5-6).

"And we know that in all things God works for the good of those who love him, who have been called according to his purpose" (Romans 8:28).

"We also glory in our sufferings, because we know that suffering produces perseverance; perseverance, character; and character, hope. And hope does not put us to shame, because God's love has been poured out into our hearts through the Holy Spirit, who has been given to us" (Romans 5:3-5).

"Because of Christ and our faith in him, we can now come boldly and confidently into God's presence" (Ephesians 3:12 NLT).

"Do not conform to the pattern of this world, but be transformed by the renewing of your mind. Then you will be able to test and approve what God's will is—his good, pleasing and perfect will" (Romans 12:2).

"SO WE CAN SAY WITH CONFIDENCE, 'THE LORD IS MY HELPER, SO I WILL HAVE NO FEAR. WHAT CAN MERE PEOPLE DO TO ME?'" (HEBREWS 13:6 NLT).

"By this everyone will know that you are my disciples, if you love one another" (John 13:35).

CHAPTER FIVE

BEING Yourself

EVEN IF EVERYONE DOESN'T LIKE YOU

You are the light of the world. A town built on a hill cannot be hidden. Neither do people light a lamp and put it under a bowl. Instead they put it on its stand, and it gives light to everyone in the house. In the same way, let your light shine before others, that they may see your good deeds and glorify your Father in heaven. Matthew 5:14-16

I GET SO EXCITED ABOUT MY SOCKS, AND I CAN'T KEEP THEM TO MYSELF.

I WANT TO SHARE THE FUN COLORS AND THE JOY I HAVE IN WEARING THEM WITH OTHER PEOPLE, SO I WEAR THEM OUTSIDE OF MY PANTS.

I want everyone to see those socks! In the same way, Jesus wants everyone to see his people. He doesn't want us to be hidden away in our homes. He said in Matthew 5:14-16, "You are the light of the world. A town built on a hill cannot be hidden. Neither do people light a lamp and put it under a bowl. Instead they put it on its stand, and it gives light to everyone in the house. In the same way, let your light shine before others, that they may see your good deeds and glorify your Father in heaven." When walking with Jesus, the joy of who he is and who I am in him cannot be held inside and was not meant to be. Wearing my socks on the outside of my pants is a reflection of me not withholding the light of Jesus, but shining his light for all to see.

WHEN WALKING WITH JESUS, THE JOY OF WHO HE IS AND WHO I AM IN HIM CANNOT BE HELD INSIDE AND WAS NOT MEANT TO BE.

When I started to walk out of the joy of the Lord that is our strength, I had a confident trust that was not in myself, but in the Lord, and this compelled me to smile so big and greet people with enthusiasm. This was and still is received in many different ways. Some people are confused and wonder if it's genuine. Some do not understand because it's so unfamiliar to them. Others have become some of my dear friends. I was able to remain steadfast in the joy of the Lord because in the depths of my heart, I truly knew that he, Yahweh, had become my shield; he took me and surrounded me with himself. His glory covered me continually. He lifted my head high when I bowed low in shame (Psalm 3:3).

EVEN IN THE MIDST OF BEING MISUNDERSTOOD AND HAVING REASONS TO FEEL REJECTED, THE LORD PROTECTED ME, AND HE ALONE WAS MY REASON TO KEEP LOVING BECAUSE I KNEW HE LOVED ME.

And in this protection, he also showed me how to respond. Jesus encouraged his disciples to "not worry about what to say or how to say it" because at that time it would not be them speaking, but the Spirit of their Father speaking through them (Matthew 10:19-20). Because of his provision and protection, I can make the most of every opportunity and choose to answer in grace and truth. Sometimes my response consisted of words and other times I listened and simply kept on walking.

Following Jesus means having the courage to be who God has called us to be. But to wholeheartedly follow Jesus we must wholeheartedly trust him. So even when people don't respond the way we would choose, we can continue to follow Jesus because his character is trustworthy. We can trust in Jesus because he knows and understands:

Inasmuch then as we
[believers] have a great
High Priest who has [already
ascended and] passed through
the heavens, Jesus the Son
of God, let us hold fast our
confession [of faith and cling
tenaciously to our absolute
trust in Him as Savior]. For
we do not have a High Priest
who is unable to sympathize
and understand our weaknesses
and temptations, but One who
has been tempted [knowing
exactly how it feels to be
human] in every respect as we
are, yet without [committing
any] sin. Therefore, let us
[with privilege] approach the
throne of grace [that is,
the throne of God's gracious
favor] with confidence and
without fear, so that we
may receive mercy [for our
failures] and find [His amazing]
grace to help in time of need
[an appropriate blessing,
coming just at the right
moment]. Hebrews 4:14-16 (AMP)

Jesus was misunderstood, laughed at, mocked, and he made the decision to trust his Father, declaring his highest good was doing his Father's will. Jesus experienced everything you will ever experience and claimed victory and freedom over it so you may trust him and rest in him and walk in the victory he claimed. To trust Jesus means that my circumstance does not determine my courage, but his constant presence is the source of my courage. Some people will like how we wear our socks on the outside of our pants, while others will not. Just as Jesus trusted his Father, we can too. But the response should not determine whether or not we keep letting our light so shine.

THE LORD SAYS to trust him with all of our heart and not to lean on our own understanding. BUT IN ALL OF OUR WAYS, submit to him and he will make our paths STRAIGHT.

In order to
WALK IN
PEACE
that surpasses all understanding,
we cannot lean on our
own understanding.

peace
and
trust
GO HAND
IN HAND.

PROVERBS 3:5-6
PHILIPPIANS 4:6-7

Some of you reading this, though, may be keeping your lights hidden underneath the bowl or keeping your socks on the inside of your pants, and I want to encourage you that the forgiveness of sin is available, and the right time to do the right thing is right now. According to Hebrews 4:14-16, Jesus has made a way to be forgiven and to be helped daily. Jesus wants to daily help us let our lights shine, and he gives us the courage to do so.

PRAY

When I am nervous about what others might think of me, help me to remember that you created me uniquely and wonderfully in your image. By living in the light of Christ, help me to live confidently as your child, free to be me.

When I am tempted to live as the world lives, renew my heart and mind. Help me to let my light shine before others, walking with the joy of Jesus.

When I am tempted to trust myself over you, convince me of your unfailing, unwavering love. Out of this love and trust, help me to greet people with enthusiasm, remaining steadfast in the joy of the Lord.

When I feel rejected or misunderstood, remind me that Jesus knows and understands me. Protect my heart with your Scripture, and help me to persevere knowing I am doing kingdom work that you have called me to.

When I feel stuck, guide me to the cross. Help me to see that forgiveness of sin is available, and the right time to do the right thing is right now. Give me the courage to let my light shine, no matter the cost.

♡ SCRIPTURE TO REMEMBER ♡

"You are the light of the world. A town built on a hill cannot be hidden. Neither do people light a lamp and put it under a bowl. Instead they put it on its stand, and it gives light to everyone in the house. In the same way, let your light shine before others, that they may see your good deeds and glorify your Father in heaven" (Matthew 5:14-16).

"Let us run with perseverance the race marked out for us, fixing our eyes on Jesus, the pioneer and perfecter of faith. For the joy set before him he endured the cross, scorning its shame, and sat down at the right hand of the throne of God" (Hebrews 12:1-2).

"THEREFORE SINCE WE HAVE A GREAT HIGH PRIEST WHO HAS ASCENDED INTO HEAVEN, JESUS THE SON OF GOD, LET US HOLD FIRMLY TO THE FAITH WE PROFESS. FOR WE DO NOT HAVE A HIGH PRIEST WHO IS UNABLE TO EMPATHIZE WITH OUR WEAKNESSES, BUT WE HAVE ONE WHO HAS BEEN TEMPTED IN EVERY WAY, JUST AS WE ARE—YET HE DID NOT SIN. LET US THEN APPROACH GOD'S THRONE OF GRACE WITH CONFIDENCE, SO THAT WE MAY RECEIVE MERCY AND FIND GRACE TO HELP US IN OUR TIME OF NEED" (HEBREWS 4:14-16).

"Trust in the LORD with all your heart and lean not on your own understanding; in all your ways submit to him, and he will make your paths straight" (Proverbs 3:5-6).

"Do not be anxious about anything, but in every situation, by prayer and petition, with thanksgiving, present your requests to God. And the peace of God, which transcends all understanding, will guard your hearts and minds in Christ Jesus" (Philippians 4:6-7).

"YOUR LOVE, LORD, REACHES TO THE HEAVENS, YOUR FAITHFULNESS TO THE SKIES. YOUR RIGHTEOUSNESS IS LIKE THE HIGHEST MOUNTAINS, YOUR JUSTICE LIKE THE GREAT DEEP" (PSALM 36:5-6).

CHAPTER SIX

SCHOOL
Work

> So then, whether you eat or drink, or whatever you do, do it all for the glory of [our great] God. 1 Corinthians 10:31 AMP

I AM A PERFECTIONIST

(I think I already mentioned that!). To me, everything,

INCLUDING MY SCHOOLWORK,

had to be done perfectly.

OR THIS WAS AT LEAST WHAT I BELIEVED TO BE TRUE.

Each word had to be written with the highest quality of handwriting, and many nights were spent staying up late to ensure every detail was wholeheartedly invested in. It's beautiful to delight in the details, and it's wonderful to be wholehearted in what we do, but it becomes unhealthy when our identity and source of worth is found in our accomplishments and level of achievements.

In the seventh grade, I remember staying up late many nights and denying my body the rest it needed so that I could get good grades. I put a lot of my worth into that ambition. Not completely, but a major part of me believed my identity was found in what I did and didn't do. Quickly I learned that if I don't choose to rest, my body will force me.

A MAJOR PART OF ME BELIEVED MY IDENTITY WAS FOUND IN WHAT I DID AND DIDN'T DO

After going to bed late and waking up early and struggling with the burden of making everything perfect, I was rundown and sick in bed for an entire week. In God's Word, King Solomon says,

"IN VAIN YOU RISE EARLY AND STAY UP LATE, TOILING FOR FOOD TO EAT—FOR HE GRANTS SLEEP TO THOSE HE LOVES." (PSALM 127:2).

One day, my math teacher saw me struggle to maintain perfect grades, and I'll never forget what she said to me.

"EMMA MAE,

I'm really excited for you to understand what

grace

really is, because it's going to be really **FREEING FOR YOU."**

After this conversation, I began to realize what grace meant. I started to see that our holy and righteous God chose to see his perfect, sinless son when he looks upon me. Forgiveness is freely available for those who know Jesus and ask him for it. God knows all the ways I fall short, and he still offers me grace and love. Jesus lived the perfect life so I don't have to, and God embraces me no matter if I fail. I found freedom in knowing I can't earn his love, because it's already graciously given to me in full. No perfect grade or failing grade could ever change that truth.

I STARTED TO ASK MYSELF, "WHAT DOES IT LOOK LIKE TO WALK IN THE GRACE I ALREADY HAVE ACCESS TO?"

By walking in this freedom, I could enjoy the process of learning and glorify God in my work—without the fear of failure or never measuring up. Jesus always measures up, and because of God's grace, I was free to enjoy school.

The Lord used my teacher's words of wisdom and continues to remind me, even today, that grace is available to me, and it never runs out. "Let us then approach God's throne of grace with confidence, so that we may receive mercy and find grace to help us in our time of need" (Hebrews 4:16).

As I began to discover freedom in Christ and walk in the sweet and powerful truth that my identity is found in him, it overflowed into my schoolwork. I learned that my work is worship to him: "So then, whether you eat or drink or whatever you do, do it all for the glory of [our great] God" (1 Corinthians 10:31 AMP). As I rested in Christ, I began to realize my schoolwork was not about me, but it was and is all about him and his glory. Tasting and seeing his truth set me free and allowed me to operate out of his grace that is sufficient. Since my identity was firmly rooted in Jesus, I no longer had to seek my value how well I performed. I began to understand the grace of Jesus what an amazing gift it is.

As I transitioned into high school, I started to notice that I struggled with procrastination. Time management was simply not a strength of mine (and that is still true, ask my parents!). Sometimes I am a little disconnected from how much time I actually have. It's easy for me to think I have more time available than I do. I am learning that worshipping the Lord does not always mean doing things that would be my first choice. For example, sometimes going to get coffee with a friend would be my first pick over doing schoolwork, but I have to say no. I love spending time with people, but it's more important to honor the Lord and the due date I have for an assignment. Going to get coffee with a friend was not a bad way to spend my time; it was a very good thing, but I had a commitment I had to remain loyal to. Sometimes glorifying the Lord looks like saying no to the good things we want to do and saying yes to the good things that probably weren't our first choice.

cappuccino

LEARNING TO WALK IN FREEDOM IS SUCH AN EXCITING JOURNEY,

and I am compelled by his love and carried by his grace. I discovered that because of who God is and who I am in him, I wanted to do my best and work wholeheartedly. Because of what Jesus came and did on my behalf, I cannot help but live purposefully and give all I have. Yet even in this, I know I am still an imperfect human and **"my flesh and my heart may fail, but God is the strength of my heart and my portion forever" (Psalm 73:26).** I know I will mess up, but in him my mind is transformed to know my identity and worth are not found in the source of my accomplishments. It has been a sweet adventure of living in freedom from perfectionism and also freedom to live for God's glory. I aim to live out of a grateful heart and only want to do my best because I know it is for the Lord. I try not to take God's grace for granted and be lazy.

Paul said, "Not that I have already obtained it [this goal of being Christlike] or have already been made perfect, but I actively press on so that I may take hold of that [perfection] for which Christ Jesus took hold of me and made me His own. Brothers and sisters, I do not consider that I have made it my own yet; but one thing I do: forgetting what lies behind and reaching forward to what lies ahead" (Philippians 3:12–13 AMP). We are called to actively press on to be all that God has called us to be and reflect him in all that we do—including our schoolwork. Rather than dwelling on all of the times I missed a due date and procrastinated, I can learn from it and reach forward to apply what I learned the next time. I can continue to move forward because I know my identity is not in whether or not I turned in something late or on time, but it is secure in Christ.

PRAY

When I'm exhausted with trying to be perfect all the time, ground me in your truth, that I would find my worth in you—not my grades, achievements, performance, friendships, popularity, or _____.

When I try to find my identity in other places apart from you, help me to rest in the perfection of Jesus, whose righteousness was placed upon me as a free gift—not what I deserved or could have earned.

When I am burdened by the tasks set before me—to be a good daughter, sister, friend, student, etc.—help me to remember that everything I do is for your glory, and my identity is firmly rooted in you. I can work for your glory and find rest in you.

When I fall short and mess up, remind me that my value is not in my performance. Give me grace to see myself the way you see me, and help me to have an obedient heart when I am called to work in areas I'm not naturally gifted in or things I would rather set aside.

When I need to say no to good things and yes to good things that aren't are my first choice, help me to remember I can still glorify you with my actions and my words. Help me to remain diligent in the purpose you have called me to.

When I am discouraged, help me to forget what lies behind and reach forward to what lies ahead (Philippians 3:13). Give me the strength to actively press on to be all you have called me to be, reflecting you in all I do.

♡SCRIPTURE TO REMEMBER♡

"SO THEN, WHETHER YOU EAT OR DRINK OR WHATEVER YOU DO, DO ALL TO THE GLORY OF [OUR GREAT] GOD" (1 CORINTHIANS 10:31 AMP).

"In vain you rise early and stay up late, toiling for food to eat-for he grants sleep to those he loves" (Psalm 127:2).

"BUT YOU ARE A CHOSEN PEOPLE, A ROYAL PRIESTHOOD, A HOLY NATION, GOD'S SPECIAL POSSESSION, THAT YOU MAY DECLARE THE PRAISES OF HIM WHO CALLED YOU OUT OF DARKNESS INTO HIS MARVELOUS LIGHT" (1 PETER 2:9).

"My dear children, I write this to you so that you will not sin. But if anybody does sin, we have an advocate with the Father-Jesus Christ, the Righteous One. He is the atoning sacrifice for our sins, and not only for ours but also for the sins of the whole world" (1 John 2:1-2).

"SINCE, THEN, YOU HAVE BEEN RAISED WITH CHRIST, SET YOUR HEARTS ON THINGS ABOVE, WHERE CHRIST IS, SEATED AT THE RIGHT HAND OF GOD. SET YOUR MINDS ON THINGS ABOVE, NOT ON EARTHLY THINGS. FOR YOU DIED, AND YOUR LIFE IS NOW HIDDEN WITH CHRIST IN GOD" (COLOSSIANS 3:1-3).

CHAPTER SEVEN

SPORTS

EVERYTHING ABOUT SOCCER WAS SO MUCH FUN TO ME.

The cleats, the shin guards, the traveling for tournaments, the daily practices,

AND THE RELATIONSHIPS THAT WERE BUILT.

Let us not grow weary or become discouraged in doing good, for at the proper time we will reap, if we do not give in. Galatians 6:9 AMP

When the field had just been freshly mowed for the season and the smell of the grass filled the air, I was always filled with anticipation and joy. I loved the adrenaline of stepping onto the field as everyone went to their positions. Soccer has been a huge blessing in my life since I was five years old. Glorifying the Lord in and through it all has been so fulfilling.

"LET US NOT GROW WEARY OR BECOME DISCOURAGED IN DOING GOOD, FOR AT THE PROPER TIME WE WILL REAP, IF WE DO NOT GIVE IN." GALATIANS 6:9 AMP

But just because I loved soccer doesn't mean that I didn't experience challenges. I wanted to play my hardest and not be concerned about what others thought, but some days that was definitely a struggle. One day at practice our coach told us to run around the field a certain number of times for a workout to finish the practice. When it came time for the last lap, I noticed girls stopping before making it to the last corner.

For a moment, I worried about what they would think about me running when they all stopped, but there is incredible power in choosing to be faithful and simply obey. Even when the outcome doesn't look like everyone else's, choosing faithfulness will lead you to lay your head down on your pillow at night with peace. And regardless of whether or not we see it, the Lord will use your faithfulness to him in the details to inspire

and stir up goodness in the hearts of those who observe. "Let us not grow weary or become discouraged in doing good, for at the proper time we will reap, if we do not give in" (Galatians 6:9 AMP). A part of not growing weary or becoming discouraged in doing good may sometimes look like running to the last corner even when there aren't many running with you.

One thing that is hard about playing sports is how much we judge ourselves and worry about what others think of us based on our athletic ability. Have you ever felt like people didn't like you, or people automatically believed they were better than you? Not because of anything they did, but just based on your own assumptions? I found myself feeling this way on the soccer field. I remember one day in particular feeling so unwanted and out of place on the field. I felt like all of the girls were far better than I was and that they didn't want me on their team. This definitely affected how I played. I found myself sometimes playing as though I was the worst on the team because that's how I thought others saw me. In Judges 6, a man named Gideon was known to be the lowest member of the lowest family of the lowest tribe in all of Israel, and he walked as though that was where his identity rested. Gideon is threshing wheat in a winepress to hide it from the enemy-who are the Midianites at the time-and he is overcome with fear. Gideon is full of fear because he believed himself to be what other people viewed him to be. The Lord approaches Gideon as he's hiding in the winepress and calls out to him by saying, "The LORD is with you, mighty warrior" (Judges 6:12).

Like Gideon,
I found my heart sometimes hidden behind the winepress

instead of resting in the truth that the Lord was with me. My team did not give me reason to believe they thought of me that way—it was just a lie I believed about myself. When we forget who God has called us to be, we let ourselves obsess over how we think others see us. It's a dangerous place to be. "For God is not a God of disorder but of peace" (1 Corinthians 14:33). When we are operating out of confusing thoughts such as banking our worth on how we think others see us, it's a guarantee that we will not have peace. The Lord called Gideon to lead an entire nation into freedom, but I wonder what would have happened if Gideon refused to believe the Lord did indeed call him "mighty warrior." As I reflect on the days I rested in who God claimed me to be, I remember being so full of encouragement for the girls around me and being overwhelmed in joy to play soccer wholeheartedly. Those were my best playing days, when I put my confident trust in the Lord rather than placing it in the assumed opinions of others.

WHEN WE FORGET WHO GOD HAS CALLED US TO BE, WE LET OURSELVES OBSESS OVER HOW WE THINK OTHERS SEE US.

Confidence in the love of God enables us to love others better than ever before because we are now operating out of an overflow of his love that never fails. "So do not throw away your confidence; it will be richly rewarded" (Hebrews 10:35). Daily I got to practice what it meant to place my confident trust in the Lord instead of pleasing others, and a part of this looked like celebrating wholeheartedly on the bench. It's beautiful how much we find out about ourselves when the attention is not on us. To sit on the bench and cheer for the girls on my team and genuinely desire the best for them because we were a team was such a sweet time of experiencing the heart of Jesus. Division can be found when members of the same team are seeking to compete with each other

DAILY

BEN CH

instead of complementing
each other's strength. When we
begin to see ourselves the way God sees
us, we can see others the way that God sees others.
Since we moved often, I was on many different soccer teams
growing up. On each team, I saw the heart of God in those precious
girls in a way that made me better. Some days I chose to not join in
conversations or sing along to the songs they were singing, but gracious, it
was such a joy to love them and learn from them and be encouraged by
them in the ways only the Lord could have orchestrated.

I got to practice what it meant to place my confident trust ___ in the Lord

As I played soccer, I was challenged to love God with my whole heart first and then to love others out of his love. That kept me from trying to just fit in because I wanted to be liked (which of course I did). "But just as he who called you is holy, so be holy in all you do; for it is written: 'Be holy, because I am holy'" (1 Peter 1:15-16). This was an anthem that God sang over my heart as I grew up playing soccer. To be his is to be set apart. Sometimes being set apart feels lonely, but there is sweet peace in knowing the Lord will never leave you and never forsake you. His presence is not determined by how we feel. The presence of the Lord is based on his promise to be with us. Although I felt alone at many practices, even while being surrounded by thirty other girls, I was reminded of Jacob as he woke up in the desert. While in his sleep, the Lord tells Jacob, "'I am with you and will watch over you wherever you go and will bring you back to this land. I will not leave you until I have done what I have promised you.' When Jacob woke up, he thought, "Surely the LORD is in this place, and I was not aware of it'" (Genesis 28:15-16).

THE
love
& *truth*
OF GOD
is not always popular.
BUT HOW UPLIFTING
is it to know the
King of Kings
IS WITH US
AND WATCHING
OVER US.

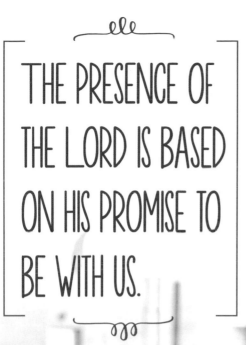

THE PRESENCE OF THE LORD IS BASED ON HIS PROMISE TO BE WITH US.

PRAY

When I'm making a decision and I'm worried what people might think of me, help me to choose truth. Even when the outcome doesn't look like everyone else's, stir my affections for you, and help me to honor you in all I do.

When I grow weary or become discouraged in doing good, help me to adopt a kingdom mind-set. Sustain me and strengthen me to continue following you where you are leading me.

When my assumptions take over or I feel like people don't like me, show me Jesus. Help me to remember my identity, and when I forget who you have called me to be, encourage me by your Spirit. Remind me your presence is not determined by how I feel.

When I make choices that aren't popular, fix my eyes on what is eternal. Help me to live out of an overflow of your love for me and see others as you see them.

When I am lacking in confidence, refresh me by your Spirit. Help me to place my confident trust in you instead of pleasing others.

♡ SCRIPTURE TO REMEMBER ♡

"Let us not grow weary or become discouraged in doing good, for at the proper time we will reap, if we do not give in" (Galatians 6:9 AMP).

"BUT JUST AS HE WHO CALLED YOU IS HOLY, SO BE HOLY IN ALL YOU DO; FOR IT IS WRITTEN: 'BE HOLY, BECAUSE I AM HOLY'" (I PETER 1:15–16).

"So do not throw away your confidence, it will be richly rewarded" (Hebrews 10:35).

"My dear children, I write this to you so that you will not sin. But if anybody does sin, we have an advocate with the Father-Jesus Christ, the Righteous One. He is the atoning sacrifice for our sins, and not only for ours but also for the sins of the whole world" (I John 2:1–2).

"SO WE FIX OUR EYES NOT ON WHAT IS SEEN, BUT ON WHAT IS UNSEEN, SINCE WHAT IS SEEN IS TEMPORARY, BUT WHAT IS UNSEEN IS ETERNAL" (2 CORINTHIANS 4:18).

"'For I know the plans I have for you,' declares the LORD, 'plans to prosper you and not to harm you, plans to give you hope and a future'" (Jeremiah 29:11).

"Let us then approach God's throne of grace with confidence, so that we may receive mercy and find grace to help us in our time of need" (Hebrews 4:16).

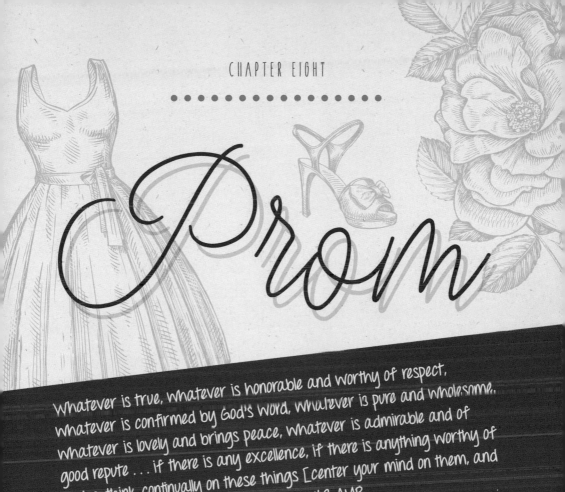

CHAPTER EIGHT

Prom

> Whatever is true, whatever is honorable and worthy of respect, whatever is confirmed by God's Word, whatever is pure and wholesome, whatever is lovely and brings peace, whatever is admirable and of good repute . . . if there is any excellence, if there is anything worthy of praise, think continually on these things [center your mind on them, and implant them in your heart]. Philippians 4:8 AMP

When I was in the tenth grade, I couldn't yet go to the prom—it was only for juniors and seniors. But when the time for prom came around, the Lord laid it on my heart to go and tell the other girls how gorgeous they were and that they were seen and valued by God. I asked my momma if she could drive me to the places where people took pictures, so I could tell everyone how special and beautiful they were. She said, "Yes." Right away I put on a ball cap, a big T-shirt, and leggings, and off we went to pour into people and speak life over them.

My momma was so willing to help me be a vessel of encouragement to all of these precious people that the Lord loves so much. They were all so pretty in their dresses, and what a joy it was to let them know! I told them they were stunning because before they were born, God knit them together in their mother's womb, fearfully and wonderfully (Psalm 139:14). We did this for a couple of hours, and I was amazed how energized I was when I wasn't focused on myself. The Word of God is full of energy, so when we are operating out of his Word, we are operating out of an energy that is led by the Spirit and not by our own strength that will grow weary. I was overwhelmed and in awe at how alive I felt to speak life over other people. It is refreshing to refresh others.

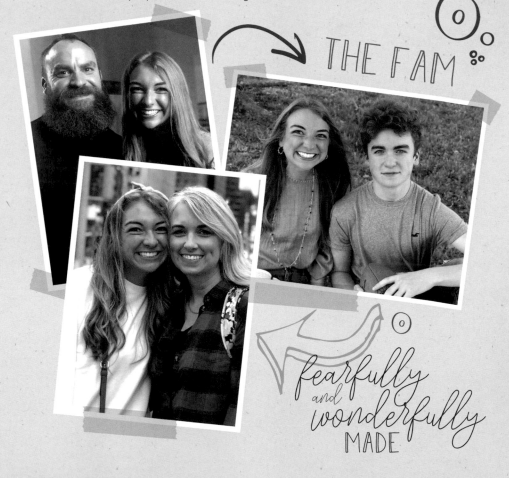

THE FAM

fearfully and wonderfully MADE

THE SECRET TO NOT BEING DISCOURAGED AND NOT COMPARING YOURSELF TO OTHERS IS OFTEN FINDING CONTENTMENT IN THE SEASON THE LORD WANTS YOU TO BE IN.

When it was my turn to go to prom, I decided that I didn't want to have a date. I just wanted to go with my friends. The Lord had laid this on my heart as what he had for me this year. There is such freedom in embracing the season God has you in. As a senior in high school, I didn't have a boyfriend. I didn't go on dates. Even though many of my classmates went on dates, I found a sweet joy in realizing the Lord had me in a season that was right for me. The secret to not being discouraged and not comparing yourself to others is often finding contentment in the season the Lord wants you to be in. For me, this was a season of investing in my friendships and remaining solid in singleness. Once you embrace this freedom, you can be content and excited for your friends that are in a different season. You can love and encourage your friends and still be content with where the Lord has you.

Though I didn't have a date, I was so excited to dress up and go to prom. My sister and I went to get our hair done at a salon, and the hair stylists were so skilled. They did my curls and Caroline's updo. Soon after, we headed over to my best friend's house, right down the street, who is a pro at doing makeup. She loves to help others see themselves as the masterpieces God made them to be. One of my favorite parts of prom was getting to include others in helping me get ready and getting to show off how good God is by highlighting the gifts he entrusted these girls with. Between the hair stylists, my sweet makeup pro pal, and my lovely momma who was a helper to me and Caroline in any way that was needed, so many different skills were put into practice on this day. It was a delight to honor these people by inviting them into positions to use their talents for good.

My dress was a beautiful blue with strokes of greens and grays, and when I put it on, I was encouraged because I was reminded of the winds and the waves. In Matthew 8, Jesus rebuked the winds and the waves, and it was completely calm. The men who were with him were amazed and asked, "what kind of man is this? Even the winds and the waves obey him!" (Matthew 8:26-27). I was reminded that we are dressed in his power and authority because "we are seated with Him in the heavenly places" (Ephesians 2:6 AMP). As I put blue velvet high heels on my feet and some Converses in the car for later, my heart smiled bigger than my face could because I was reminded of how we are "fitted with the readiness that comes from the gospel of peace" (Ephesians 6:15).

Picking up the flower crown that bloomed in the most vibrant yellows and pinks and oranges and greens, I placed it on my head and rejoiced in "whatever is true, whatever is honorable and worthy of respect, whatever is confirmed by God's Word, whatever is pure and wholesome, whatever is lovely and brings peace, whatever is admirable and of good repute . . . if there is any excellence, if there is anything worthy of praise, think continually on these things [center your mind on them, and implant them in your heart]" (Philippians 4:8 AMP).

Once we were all ready to rock and roll, we headed off to take pictures, eat yummy food, and go to the prom. My sister and I danced and sang and laughed as we repeatedly told each other how beautiful the other was and ate chicken nuggets. There is gladness in speaking life over one another. It's outstanding how when we begin to fill ourselves with God's Word, we begin to see his Word in all that we see, even in the details of flower crowns, blue velvet shoes, and ocean-colored dresses. He delights in the details of our lives, and when we begin to have an awareness of his delight, joy that is "inexpressible and glorious" will overflow our cups (1 Peter 1:8).

THERE IS GLADNESS IN SPEAKING LIFE OVER ONE ANOTHER.

He delights in the DETAILS of our lives

Always be prepared to give AN ANSWER to everyone FOR THE HOPE THAT WE HAVE.

We had such a fun night together. It turns out that I didn't need a date to have a great time at prom. But one thing that helped me to glorify God in all that fun was having a game plan going in. At any dance, people might invite you to do things that do not glorify the Lord. But prom does seem more intense that way. Sometimes we say yes to doing things we don't really want to do, because we don't know how to say no, or we're afraid of what people will think of us if we do say no. I have found that the best strategy is to think about that ahead of time and have an answer prepared before the situation finds you. In 1 Peter 3:15, we are encouraged to "always be prepared to give an answer to everyone for the hope that [we] have. But do this with gentleness and respect."

BUT DO THIS WITH GENTLENESS AND RESPECT.

1 PETER 3:15

SOMETIMES WHAT LOOKS LIKE REJECTION WILL TURN INTO AN INVITATION.

Those who receive your rejection to doing something you know dishonors the Lord may question why you were so confident in him, and it could eventually lead them to seek and find him, "though he is not far from any of us" (Acts 17:27). It was a wise move for me to go to prom with a group of friends who were like-minded and confident in seeking to glorify God, enjoying the dance without feeling as though we had to do things that seemed popular or cool at the time. "Bad company corrupts good morals" (1 Corinthians 15:33 AMP), and so major significance is found in who I choose to go with. To walk hand in hand with Jesus is not to miss out on all of the "fun" but rather to be protected for the best and most freeing fun that nothing in this world can provide. Never does he settle on us, for he surely knows what is best and because of that we can trust in the Lord with all of our hearts and not lean on our own understanding, but in all of our ways acknowledge him, and he will make our paths straight (Proverbs 3:5–6). "Be alert and of sober mind. Your enemy the devil prowls around like a roaring lion looking for someone to devour. Resist him, standing firm in the faith" (1 Peter 5:8–9). We can be alert and of sober mind by spending time in his word and preparing our hearts to give an answer at any time—and by surrounding ourselves with godly people who will encourage us in truth.

God's grace
is sufficient
for you

We have all said yes to some things that have been offered to us that did break the heart of God. Regardless of what your reasoning for saying yes was, God's "grace is sufficient for you" (2 Corinthians 12:9), and when we draw near to him, he will draw near to us and forgive us of our sins (James 4:8). To be a Christian doesn't mean to be perfect. It's about a relationship with him, and to be in relationship with him means we will grow into desiring what the Lord desires. We won't always walk that out perfectly, but we seek to glorify him because he is worthy, and he calls us to be holy because he is holy. To follow Jesus means we must daily deny ourselves and pick up our cross.

This looks like saying no to what the world invites us into and saying yes to the exceedingly and abundantly greater things that God has in store for us because he loves us.

LUKE 9:23;
EPHESIANS 3:20;
1 PETER 1:16

PRAY

When I am tempted to only care about myself and my own comforts and desires, give me compassion for the people around me, and help me to remind them that they are seen and valued by God. Help me to remember there is gladness in speaking life over others.

When I'm feeling overwhelmed, show me how you delight in the details of my life. Help me to respond with joy to those around me.

When I am tempted to make a choice that could hurt you or those around me, help me to remember that your grace is sufficient for all things. Draw near to me and forgive me for my sins. Give me the strength to repent and turn toward you.

When I'm stuck on what's temporary, help me to deny myself, pick up my cross, and follow you. Help me to say no to what the world invites me into and yes to the exceedingly and abundantly greater things you have in store for me.

When I need wisdom, lead me to the cross. Help me to be alert and of sober mind, and don't let me lean on my own understanding but stand firm in my faith (Proverbs 3:5).

❧ SCRIPTURE TO REMEMBER ❧

"Finally, believers, whatever is true, whatever is honorable and worthy of respect, whatever is right and confirmed by God's word, whatever is pure and wholesome, whatever is lovely and brings peace, whatever is admirable and of good repute; if there is any excellence, if there is anything worthy of praise, think continually on these things [center your mind on them, and implant them in your heart]" (Philippians 4:8 AMP).

"THOUGH YOU HAVE NOT SEEN HIM, YOU LOVE HIM; AND EVEN THOUGH YOU DO NOT SEE HIM NOW, YOU BELIEVE IN HIM AND ARE FILLED WITH INEXPRESSIBLE AND GLORIOUS JOY" (1 PETER 1:8).

"But in your hearts revere Christ as Lord. Always be prepared to give an answer to everyone who asks you to give the reason for the hope that you have. But do this with gentleness and respect" (1 Peter 3:15).

"TRUST IN THE LORD WITH ALL YOUR HEART AND LEAN NOT ON YOUR OWN UNDERSTANDING; IN ALL YOUR WAYS SUBMIT TO HIM, AND HE WILL MAKE YOUR PATHS STRAIGHT" (PROVERBS 3:5–6).

"Be alert and of sober mind. Your enemy the devil prowls around like a roaring lion looking for someone to devour. Resist him, standing firm in the faith, because you know that the family of believers throughout the world is undergoing the same kind of sufferings" (1 Peter 5:8-9).

"The LORD directs the steps of the godly. He delights in every detail of their lives" (Psalm 37:23 NLT).

At the beginning of
senior year, the entire senior class
had the opportunity to vote for
eight senior homecoming maids
who would be on court.
Our senior class had about 750
world-changing students.

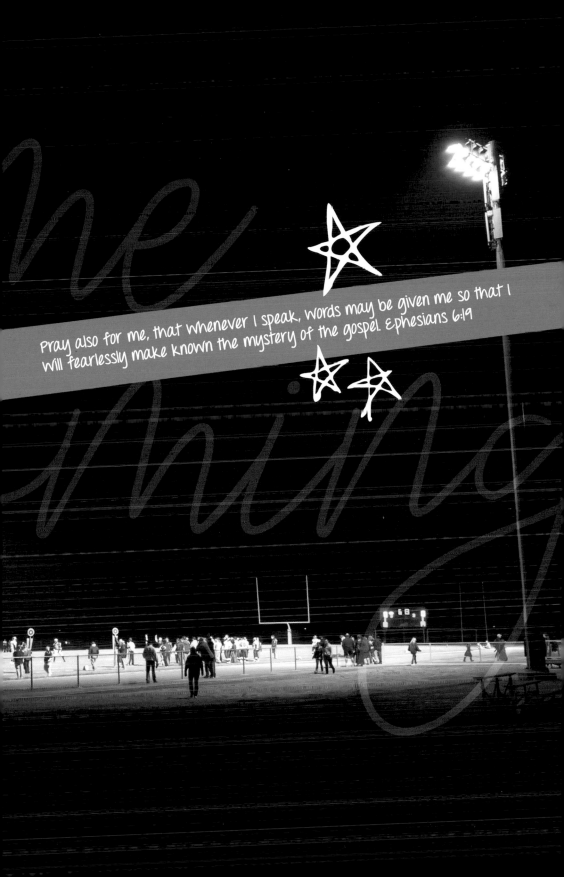

Pray also for me, that whenever I speak, words may be given me so that I will fearlessly make known the mystery of the gospel. Ephesians 6:19

The day the names were made known, I remember asking a friend of mine who all of the maids were because I wanted to go on and congratulate them. My friend responded by telling me seven names, but she said she didn't know who the eighth girl was. Then one of the leaders of student council came up to me with a folded piece of paper in her hand. As she gave it to me, she congratulated me for being voted on court. I was the eighth girl. In awe, I stood in humility. "Humble yourselves, therefore, under God's mighty hand, that he may lift you up in due time" (1 Peter 5:6), because he lifts us up to lift him higher, and he places us in positions where he entrusts us with his name.

IT IS SO SWEET GETTING TO BE AN
ATTENTION REDIRECTOR.
As children of God,
WE ARE CALLED TO REDIRECT
THE FOCUS & ATTENTION
TO THE ONE
WHO IS WORTHY
OF IT ALL.

On the morning of homecoming, I got up as I always do very early in the morning to be with Jesus and read John 19.
I didn't plan on reading this chapter on that particular morning, but it was where I was in my time with him.

In John 19,

Jesus is about to be crucified, and the Roman "soldiers twisted together a crown of thorns to put on his head. They clothed him in a purple robe and went up to him again and again, saying, 'Hail, king of the Jews!' And they slapped him in the face" (John 19:2–3). I thought about how much he loves us, to be treated like that for our sakes. I walked into that day captivated by the heart of my God.

The morning of the homecoming game we had a pep rally, and before the rally I had a chance to look back and remember the faithfulness of God. I thought about when I first moved to Arkansas and was scared about whether or not I was going to connect with people. I laughed at that fear as I prepared to stand in my homecoming ball gown, in front of the entire student body as student body president and give a speech about the love of Christ. I stood at the podium, in front of every freshman, sophomore, junior, and senior, excited to the core about the good, pleasing, and perfect will that the Lord has for each of them, and simply opened my mouth. Paul prayed in Ephesians 6 that words may be given to him so that he may boldly make known the mystery of the gospel (v. 19). It wasn't his own words he wanted, but words given to him by the Spirit speaking through him. When we come to the Lord with a pure heart of wanting to know him and make him known, he will give us the words to speak. We simply need to be willing to open our mouth because we are his ambassadors.

Before the evening game, the sun began to rest as the Lord spoke vibrant beauty into the sky to create a canvas of pinks and golds and blues and purples. I love how he woos us with his love through every moment, like the bursts of life and love in the sky as the sun brings daytime to the other side of the earth. My daddy, who would be escorting me, looked handsome in his blazer and rocked his beard so well. With the purest joy, my heart exploded as I put my blue, embroidered dress on. My exquisite momma helped me get ready and a lovely pal of mine who lived down the street from me did my makeup (just like she did for prom!).

I LOVE HOW HE WOOS US
WITH HIS LOVE THROUGH
EVERY MOMENT

We drove to the football field so excited about how God was going to be glorified that night.

All of the maids looked beautiful in their gowns, and it was so fun getting to see them and celebrate with them. Before the game started, they had all eight of us line up with our dads on the visitor side of the football field. One by one, they called each of us to walk out on the field. I felt such a sweet security as I stood there with my daddy knowing my heavenly Daddy was also standing right there with me upholding me, delighted to escort me.

When they called my name, I couldn't contain my smile. For the entire walk down the field Daddy J and I laughed and laughed in thankfulness and goofy gladness. After all of us had been escorted to our places on the field, we waited as the announcer built up the moment of revealing who the 2017 Homecoming Queen was going to be. I stood with my arm on my daddy's strong right arm as they called my name! My jaw dropped, and my daddy kissed my cheek and gave me a high five as we rejoiced together. Flowers were given to me as my daddy crowned me. How sweet it was to be holding those flowers. "See how the flowers of the field grow" because if our heavenly Daddy takes care of the flowers of the field, won't he indeed take care of us (Matthew 6:28)?

I didn't know what to say, so I praised God in my heart and smiled so big because I knew this was all about him.

I had a sleepover that night with one of my best friends, and as we were falling asleep, I told her about what I had read in John that morning. We both became overjoyed as we realized what the Lord was telling us.

JESUS

WAS CROWNED WITH THORNS SO WE COULD BE CROWNED IN

ETERNAL LIFE

THAT IS ABUNDANT."

Just as my daddy crowned me and rejoiced over me, our heavenly Father rejoices over us and crowns us with life. "For God so loved the world that he gave his one and only Son, that whoever believes in him shall not perish but have eternal life. For God did not send his Son to condemn the world, but to save the world through him" (John 3:16-17). Often we find ourselves settling in our struggles and justifying our sin, but Jesus did not die on the cross to free us and save us so we could just survive and make it through life. No, he came so we may "have and enjoy life, and have it in abundance [to the full, till it overflows]" (John 10:10 AMP). We can live loved because we have been set free and robed in righteousness by the blood of Jesus and crowned in life that's found in the life he lives because he defeated death. For if you embrace the truth, it will release true freedom into your lives (John 8:32). For freedom we have been set free, so let's not be yoked again by another burden of slavery (Galatians 5:1). We are his royal priesthood, and Jesus was slapped in the face so our faces may be lifted up with his glory (Psalm 3:3; John 19:3). For "those who look to him are radiant; their faces are never covered with shame" (Psalm 34:5).

WE CAN LIVE LOVED BECAUSE WE HAVE BEEN SET FREE AND ROBED IN RIGHTEOUSNESS BY THE BLOOD OF JESUS

PRAY

When I receive good gifts, help me to be an attention redirector. Help me to turn my focus on you, the one who is worthy of all attention and praise. Remind me how you are working out your good, pleasing, and perfect will for me.

When I need to remember your promises, open my eyes to see how you've worked and are working in my life. Thank you for rejoicing over me and crowning me with life.

When I'm tempted to justify my sin or settle in my struggles, capture my heart by your Word. Remind me that you came to give me abundant, full life, and I can walk in freedom because of the righteousness of Jesus.

When I feel shame, point me to Jesus, who died for my sin, shame, and guilt that I might be invited into the family of God. Help me to experience true freedom because of this truth.

When I'm afraid you will keep good things from me, remind my heart of all that you've freely given to me. Help me to know you love and cherish me as your daughter, and nothing can separate me from your love.

❧ SCRIPTURE TO REMEMBER ❧

"Humble yourselves, therefore, under God's mighty hand, that he may lift you up in due time" (1 Peter 5:6).

"For God so loved the world that he gave his one and only Son, that whoever believe in him shall not perish but have eternal life. For God did not send his Son into the world to condemn the world, but to save the world through him" (John 3:16-17).

"THEN YOU WILL KNOW THE TRUTH, AND THE TRUTH WILL SET YOU FREE" (JOHN 8:32).

"the thief comes only to steal and kill and destroy; I have come that they may have life, and have it to the full" (John 10:10).

"And why do you worry about clothes? See how the flowers of the field grow. They do not labor or spin. Yet I tell you that not even Solomon in all his splendor was dressed like one of these. If that is how God clothes the grass of the field, which is here today and tomorrow is thrown into the fire, will he not much more clothe you — you of little faith?" (Matthew 6:28).

"It is for freedom that Christ has set us free. Stand firm, then, and do not let yourselves be burdened again by a yoke of slavery" (Galatians 5:1).

CHAPTER TEN

BE LOVED.

Be You.

I WAS NOT MADE TO LOOK
LIKE YOU AND YOU WERE
NOT MADE TO LOOK LIKE ME
WE'RE ALL MADE TO LOOK
LIKE JESUS

God has said, "Never will I leave you; never will I forsake you." So we say
with confidence, "The Lord is my helper; I will not be afraid" (Hebrews 13:5-6).

God has made each of us so beautifully different and has set us apart in his image for such a time as this (Genesis 1:27; Esther 4:14; Jeremiah 1:5). Fearfully and wonderfully, he knit you together in your mother's womb and your frame was not hidden from him when you were made in the secret place and woven together in the depths of the earth. His eyes saw your unformed body, and he ordained every day of your life in his book before one of them came to be (Psalm 139:13-16). He custom-makes each of us with different personalities and places and purposes, and it is all done intentionally to glorify him.

I will give thanks and praise to You for I am fearfully and wonderfully made

PSALM 139:14

IT'S BEAUTIFUL
HOW SIMPLY
BEING WHO GOD
HAS CALLED US
TO BE BRINGS
HIM GLORY.

HOW AM I UNIQUE?

Sometimes I'm goofy and ask questions that will make my family sometimes turn around and wonder if I truly did just ask that question. Pure laughter overflows as we share what my family has given the title **Emma Moments**. They are beautiful. I don't have the ability to dance in a way that will compel judges to give me a ten-out-of-ten score, but my gracious, I enjoy dancing with my whole heart. You already know I like to wear my socks on the outside of my pants, and I rarely wear clothes that would match according to a lot of people.

WHAT ELSE?

I love being with people,
it's energizing and sweet and fun to
sit with people and listen to them and
encourage them in truth. Even if not
a single word is spoken, just to be with
them is a gift, but I also love to escape
in my secret place with the Lord—
just me and him—quite often.

And here is something about myself I don't even understand—I still have not opened up packages that I received in the mailroom last week, and I can't tell you exactly why. It's awesome to have a joyful confidence in the quirks God delighted to create in each of us.

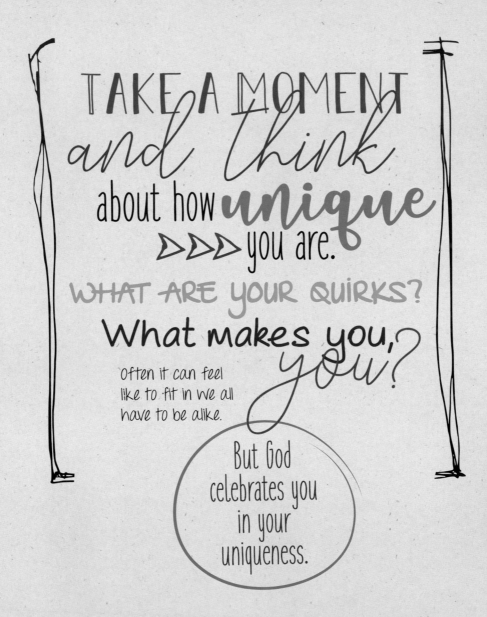

TAKE A MOMENT

and think

about how unique

▷▷▷ you are.

WHAT ARE YOUR QUIRKS?

What makes you,

you?

Often it can feel like to fit in we all have to be alike.

But God celebrates you in your uniqueness.

It's only in the Lord that we can truly discover who we were made to be, and when our identity is discovered in him, we can freely walk in it without comparing our personalities to the personalities of others.

We are each in different places in life and the Lord sees us in that place. The Lord says, "'Never will I leave you nor forsake you.' So, we say with confidence, 'The Lord is my helper; I will not be afraid'" (Hebrews 13:5-6).

BECAUSE HE IS OUR HELPER

in these different places, we can make the most of every opportunity even in difficulty. Our different places can look like challenges in our families, illnesses, broken relationships, or even moving from one place to another. The Lord promises he is working all things together for the good of those who love him and are called according to his purpose (Romans 8:28). Knowing how to be content no matter what your place or circumstance comes from trusting that you can do all things through Christ who gives us strength (Philippians 4:13).

NO PLACE IS TOO HARD FOR HIM TO BRING LIGHT TO,

When adopting this confident trust in the Lord, we will begin to see God wants to use our specific personalities to shine his light into the place he put us. This can only be done with the help of the Spirit. Ask for the Spirit's help-you can't make it without him! Being empowered by the Spirit, I can be all that he has called me to be and be a vessel of his life in any place I am presently standing in.

REDEEM, OR HEAL. HE WILL NOT WASTE YOUR PLACE.

In Ephesians 4:1, Paul encourages the people of Ephesus with this

"So I, the prisoner for the Lord, appeal to you to live a life worthy of the calling to which you have been called [that is, to live a life that exhibits godly character, moral courage, personal integrity, and mature behavior—a life that expresses gratitude to God for your salvation]" (AMP).

I love how living our purpose looks like living out of a grateful heart for what Jesus did on the cross for us. We can only live out our purpose—a life of praise to God through our personalities and our place—with the help of the Holy Spirit. Before Jesus went back to heaven to sit at the right hand of the Father, he told his disciples, "You will receive power and ability when the Holy Spirit comes upon you; and you will be My witnesses [to tell all people about Me] both in Jerusalem and in all Judea, and in Samaria, and even to the ends of the earth" (Acts 1:8 AMP).

My senior year, I was an office assistant, and I would sit in the office early in the mornings before my first class of the day. One night, I got out some flash cards and wrote encouragements and gospel truth. The next morning in the office, I asked the counselor if I could go to the bathroom. I was so excited to tape all of these flash cards full of encouragements on the bathroom mirrors. I knew that for some girls, looking in the mirror every day led to thinking negative things about themselves. How powerful would it be to give them words of love and encouragement to read while looking at their reflection? Living my purpose in the place God has me means being obedient to the simple things. When we live out our unique calling, God uses the small, seemingly insignificant things and multiples them for kingdom investment.

LIVING MY PURPOSE IN THE PLACE GOD HAS ME MEANS BEING OBEDIENT TO THE SIMPLE THINGS.

I can only be who
God has called me
to be and embrace
the beautiful and
intentional personality
he has entrusted
to me.

I choose to be fully present and trusting in the place he has me and walk in the purpose he's given me with the help of the Holy Spirit who lives within me. "My flesh and my heart may fail, but God is the strength of my heart and my portion forever" (Psalm 73:26). "It is God who arms me with strength and keeps my way secure" (2 Samuel 22:33). The Spirit has made his home in my heart and speaks to me through the Word that is truth and sets me free and leads me on level ground (Psalm 143:10; John 8:32). When I don't know what to pray, he intercedes for me with wordless groans according to the will of the Father (Romans 8:26-27). He gives us everything we need for a godly life through our knowledge of him who called us by his own glory and goodness (2 Peter 1:3). God reminds me daily of my identity and guides me to those who he wants to help through me. We cannot do it without him, and he is worthy of all the glory.

My prayer for you, as you read this book, is that you will also want to live for Christ and trust your heavenly Father through the work of his Spirit in all things and for all things. Jesus has never failed me. He will never fail you. He loves you and wants you to grow closer to him. And the best part? He will give you his Spirit to help you. "I will not leave you as orphans; I will come to you" (John 14:18). When you come to Jesus and ask forgiveness for your sins, you belong to him. Nothing can snatch you out of his hands (John 10:28).

∞ PRAY ∞

When I am tempted to compare myself to others, remind me that I am not made to look like anyone else, but that we're all made to look like Jesus. Help me to believe I am fearfully and wonderfully made in your image—and remind me that you've given me a unique personality, place, and purpose.

When I struggle to know who I am, give me a joyful confidence in the quirks you delighted to create in me. Help me discover who I was personally made to be so I can walk freely without comparison or insecurities.

When I am in a difficult place in life—physical or situational—help me to know you see me and meet me in that place. You are my helper, and I have no reason to fear. Remind me that you promise to work all things together for the good of those who love you and are called according to your purpose (Romans 8:28).

When I struggle to be content in my circumstances, help me to adopt a confident trust in you. Remind me that no place is too hard for you to bring light to, redeem, or heal. You will not waste my place.

When I forget my purpose—a life of praise to you through my personalities and my place—remind me that I am already redeemed and called your daughter. Thank you for giving me everything I need for a godly life through your Holy Spirit.

SCRIPTURE TO REMEMBER

"And we know that in all things God works for the good of those who love him, who have been called according to his purpose" (Romans 8:28).

"I CAN DO ALL THIS THROUGH HIM WHO GIVES ME STRENGTH" (PHILIPPIANS 4:13).

"SO WE SAY WITH CONFIDENCE, 'THE LORD IS MY HELPER; I WILL NOT BE AFRAID. WHAT CAN MERE MORTALS DO TO ME?'" (HEBREWS 13:6).

"His divine power has given us everything we need for a godly life through our knowledge of him who called us by his own glory and goodness" (2 Peter 1:3).

"You are worthy, our lord and God, to receive glory and honor and power, for you created all things, and by your will they were created and have their being" (Revelation 4:11).

"For you created my inmost being; you knit me together in my mother's womb. I praise you because I am fearfully and wonderfully made" (Psalm 139:13 14).